Original title:
Love's Lingering Lessons

Copyright © 2024 Swan Charm
All rights reserved.

Author: Paula Raudsepp
ISBN HARDBACK: 978-9916-86-584-2
ISBN PAPERBACK: 978-9916-86-585-9
ISBN EBOOK: 978-9916-86-586-6

Pillars of Time's Embrace

Silent shadows stretch and sway,
Beneath the weight of countless days.
Ancient stones, in stillness found,
Holding secrets in the ground.

Whispers drift through aged halls,
Echoing the past's soft calls.
Each moment, a fragile thread,
Woven where the wise have tread.

Gardens bloom with stories old,
In the sunlight, they unfold.
Memories whisper, soft yet clear,
Time embraces, drawing near.

Laughter lingers, joy and pain,
In the dance of sun and rain.
Each heartbeat, a fleeting sign,
In the pillars, hearts align.

Seasons change but still they stand,
Guardians of a timeless land.
In their shade, we find our place,
Resting in time's warm embrace.

Whispers on a Dusty Shelf

Forgotten tomes in quiet rows,
Each spine tells tales that nobody knows.
Dust motes dance in shafts of light,
Carrying stories into the night.

Pages yellowed with age and care,
Breathe the secrets hidden there.
Ancient ink, a timeless sigh,
In the silence, voices lie.

Faded covers wear their grace,
Each one holds a cherished place.
Whispers linger, soft and low,
In the stillness, memories flow.

Once embraced in eager hands,
Now they rest on quiet stands.
Yet in shadows, dreams await,
For curious hearts to desecrate.

Time may bury what once was bright,
But every whisper holds a light.
On dusty shelves where stories dwell,
We find our truths, hear the bell.

The Value of Distant Echoes

Faintest sound from far away,
Calls to us in a gentle sway.
Echoes linger, soft and clear,
Reminding us of what we dear.

Voices carried on the breeze,
Speak of distant memories.
Each note a thread in life's vast loom,
Binding hearts with joy and gloom.

Time wears on, yet still they sing,
Whispers of what the moments bring.
In their tones, the past is found,
A cherished song in every sound.

Across the years, they weave their cast,
Moments captured, memories past.
In silence, we hear the call,
Distant echoes unite us all.

Value lies in what we hear,
In echoes drawing ever near.
For every moment that's gone by,
Lives in echoes that refuse to die.

The Anatomy of Longing

In quiet rooms where shadows play,
A whisper lingers, hearts in sway.
Threads of dreams weave through the night,
Echoing hopes, a faded light.

Each sigh a story, yet untold,
Masking wishes, bold yet cold.
Time drips slowly, a quiet stream,
Beneath the surface, lies the dream.

Glimmers of laughter, distant sounds,
Clutching memories, time unbounds.
Fingers stretched in the empty air,
Reaching for moments, always rare.

In the silence, longing grows,
A tender ache that softly flows.
Beyond the touch, beyond the sight,
Lies the yearning for what feels right.

So here we stand, hearts laid bare,
In the anatomy of despair.
Chasing shadows, we find our way,
Longing fuels the night and day.

Silhouettes of a Forgotten Touch

In moonlight's glow, the past appears,
Silhouettes formed from hidden years.
Where laughter once danced in the air,
Now echoes linger, a silent prayer.

Fingers brushed in secret places,
Traces lost in timeless spaces.
A fleeting glance, a stolen sigh,
Moments cherished, yet they pass by.

The clock ticks softly, memories fade,
In the stillness, love's cascade.
Ghostly figures haunt the mind,
Remnants of what we left behind.

Each reminder pulls us again,
To whispered dreams held by the rain.
Yet here I stand, with open arms,
Enveloped in your ghostly charms.

For though the touch is long since gone,
Its essence lingers, carries on.
In shadows cast by love's embrace,
We find the beauty in time's grace.

Chasing Fleeting Moments

Time slips through fingers like sand,
A dance of dreams we can't withstand.
In breaths unheld, we find our fate,
Chasing moments before they're late.

The sunrise kisses the morning dew,
A fleeting glance of something new.
Laughter bursts in vibrant hues,
Each second a treasure, a life to choose.

But shadows grow with the setting sun,
Reminding us of battles won.
Yet here we are, so alive, so bold,
Chasing memories as they unfold.

Every heartbeat, a ticking clock,
Moments captured, yet they mock.
In the rush, we find our peace,
A fleeting joy that can't be leased.

Let's hold on tight to every spark,
In the brief light against the dark.
For though the moment cannot stay,
In fleeting glory, we find a way.

The Silent Music of Us

In quiet corners where shadows dance,
Lies a melody, a whispered chance.
The silent music sways the night,
Binding souls in a gentle light.

Each heartbeat plays a subtle tune,
Beneath the stars, beneath the moon.
Unseen rhythms draw us near,
A symphony of hope and fear.

In tender glances, notes collide,
An orchestra where love abides.
With every breath, the magic flows,
In stillness, the sweetest music grows.

A lullaby of dreams we share,
In every moment, everywhere.
Through silence, vibrant chords take flight,
The music of us, a cherished light.

So let us dance, though none may see,
To the silent music, just you and me.
In harmony's embrace, we trust,
As love's pure song catches the dust.

Remnants of a Shared Dream

In whispered tones, we sailed the night,
Chasing shadows, lost in flight.
Fragments linger, soft and bright,
Echoes linger, hearts take flight.

Stars above, they guide our way,
Fading specters, come what may.
In the quiet, memories lay,
Wishing for just one more day.

Through the mist, we found our thread,
Woven stories, softly said.
Each heartbeat like a gentle tread,
Dreams once vivid, now in shreds.

Time cascades like autumn leaves,
Holding close what the heart believes.
In each loss, a love perceives,
Remnants left, as the heart grieves.

Yet in stillness, hope survives,
In every end, a dream arrives.
For in memories, our spirit thrives,
In remnants of what once was lives.

A Canvas of Unfading Colors

Brushes paint the world anew,
With strokes of joy and sorrow too.
In every hue, a tale to view,
A canvas blooms, vibrant and true.

Golden rays of morning light,
Soft pastels in the fading night.
Every shade with pure delight,
Colors dance, a wondrous sight.

On the edges, shadows creep,
Yet in beauty, secrets keep.
In every corner, dreams will leap,
A tapestry, the heart will reap.

Voices whisper through the trees,
In the rustle of the gentle breeze.
Nature's song, a melody that frees,
A canvas of life, in perfect ease.

Though colors fade, memories stay,
Imprinted art that won't decay.
In our hearts, they find their way,
A canvas bright, come what may.

Reflections in an Empty Glass

Glimmers dance, the light cascades,
In the silence, a memory fades.
Echoes linger in the shades,
Reflections lost, a heart invades.

In the depths, a story lies,
A lingering gaze, where truth belies.
Chasing dreams in muted sighs,
Fragile moments, time's disguise.

As shadows stretch across the floor,
Empty whispers speak of more.
Each sip, a tale we can't ignore,
In the quiet, feelings pour.

Cracks that form beneath the weight,
In fragile glass, we contemplate.
Every drop, a choice, a fate,
Reflections clear, but love can wait.

Through the glass, we seek the light,
Finding courage in the night.
In our hearts, we'll take the flight,
Reflections hold, our souls ignite.

Ink-Stained Memories

Pages worn, with tales untold,
Ink-stained hearts, a love so bold.
Written in whispers, dreams unfold,
Memories cherished, never cold.

Each letter forms a gentle embrace,
In every line, we find our place.
Stories linger, time won't erase,
Ink-stained memories, a tender trace.

Fleeting moments, caught on the page,
Captured souls, a timeless stage.
In the ink, we turn the age,
Cherished tales, we won't disengage.

With every drop, our lives align,
Stories woven, hearts entwine.
Through ink's flow, the past will shine,
In memories deep, forever mine.

Though pages may yellow, words remain,
Ink-stained echoes of joy and pain.
In the heart, the stories gain,
Memories bound, like love's sweet chain.

In the Shadow of Forgotten Hopes

Once vibrant dreams now gather dust,
Whispers echo where light once thrived.
In corners dark, ambitions rust,
Time's gentle hand has left them deprived.

Silent shadows dance on the wall,
Mirroring wishes that faded away.
Each heartbeat soft, a muted call,
As memories wane in shades of gray.

Cracked reflections of who we were,
Shimmering fragments in the night.
Yet still, there's a spark, a quiet stir,
Beneath the remnants of lost light.

Hope, though faded, will not die,
In the heart's chamber, it still resides.
From ashes, new dreams can surely fly,
In the silence, the soul confides.

So let us breathe, and dare to dream,
In the shadows, we find our way.
For from the depths, we shall redeem,
The forgotten hopes of yesterday.

The Art of Letting Go

Leaves fall gently from the trees,
Carried by the wind's soft song.
In the stillness, a whisper frees,
Telling us it's time to move along.

Memories cling like morning dew,
Fragile, yet they weigh us down.
In the quiet, we must break through,
Find our peace when the sun has crowned.

Letting go is a tender art,
A dance that flows with grace and ease.
With every end, a brand new start,
In the letting, we find our peace.

Chains that bind us start to fray,
As we embrace the ebb and flow.
In surrender, night turns to day,
Freedom whispers, "It's time to go."

So take a breath, and set it free,
Watch it soar beyond the sky.
In the letting, we find the key,
To live, to love, to simply try.

Stars That Still Flicker

In the vastness of the night sky,
Stars whisper tales of long ago.
Though some may bathe in darkness, shy,
Others flicker still, with a gentle glow.

They remind us of the light we seek,
Even when shadows threaten to stay.
Each tiny spark, a voice unique,
Guiding lost souls along their way.

Through storms of doubt and waves of fear,
These flickering lights refuse to fade.
With every heartbeat, they draw near,
Offering warmth when hope's delayed.

So we gaze upwards with yearning eyes,
Finding strength in the celestial dance.
For in their flicker, wisdom lies,
Encouraging each courageous chance.

Let their brightness fill your heart's space,
For in darkness, they weave their thread.
In every twinkle, find your grace,
Stars remind us we are not misled.

Dreams That Danced in Distant Light

Once upon a distant shore,
Dreams took flight on winds of chance.
With colors bright, they aimed for more,
In the glow of the night, they pranced.

Each vision spun a story bold,
Woven deep within the mind.
In the silence, they would unfold,
Revealing paths we yearned to find.

As twilight drapes the world in gold,
Hopes evolve beneath the stars.
In every heartbeat, dreams retold,
Creating magic, mending scars.

Though miles away, they still ignite,
A spark within the soul's embrace.
For dreams that danced in distant light,
Illuminate the hidden space.

So close your eyes and dare to see,
Where wishes linger, truly bright.
In every moment, let it be,
The dreams will guide you through the night.

Time's Gentle Caress

Whispers of dawn brush the sky,
Moments drift like clouds so high.
In the stillness, dreams unfold,
Time's embrace, a story told.

Shadows dance as daylight fades,
Echoes linger where love wades.
Softly the hours slip away,
In your arms, I long to stay.

Raindrops glisten on fresh ground,
In each heartbeat, solace found.
Seasons change, yet we remain,
In the warmth, we beat the pain.

Through the years, a gentle flow,
Sunlit paths where memories grow.
Hand in hand, we brave the night,
Time's gentle touch, our guiding light.

As we forge a journey vast,
Moments cherished, memories cast.
With every sigh, the future calls,
In time's embrace, love never falls.

The Spaces Between Our Words

Silence speaks when voices fade,
Unseen bonds that we have made.
In the gaps where thoughts reside,
Hidden truths and dreams collide.

Glimmers shared in fleeting glances,
Unraveled tales in quiet dances.
In the pause, the heart connects,
In the silence, love reflects.

Every laugh, a bridge we build,
In the stillness, hearts are filled.
Unvoiced hopes and soft regrets,
In these spaces, no one forgets.

Emotions sparked, a tender trace,
In the quiet, we find our place.
With every breath, our souls enlist,
In the void, it's you I miss.

Words may fail when feelings grow,
Yet in the silence, we both know.
In the depths where whispers guide,
The spaces between us coincide.

Kaleidoscope of Tomorrow

Colors blend in twilight's glow,
Dreams take flight in evening's flow.
Visions twist and turn anew,
In this dance, we chase our view.

Fragments sparkling, lights collide,
Infinite paths where hopes reside.
Through the lens of fleeting time,
We weave our tales in rhythm and rhyme.

Time's canvas, rich and wide,
Every heartbeat, a shifting tide.
Patterns swirl, a vibrant thread,
In each moment, nothing's dead.

Tomorrow whispers, brave and clear,
Guiding us through hope and fear.
In the future's embrace, we find,
A kaleidoscope of heart and mind.

Every dream a painted hue,
Reflecting what we long to do.
With each dawn, a brand-new song,
Within this world, we all belong.

Frayed Threads of Connection

Worn-out ties that bind us close,
In the fray, we see what flows.
Through the tangles, hearts still ache,
Fragile bonds that we must take.

Every thread, a tale to tell,
In the weave, we rise and fell.
Hope may fray but won't let go,
In connection's depth, we grow.

Moments shared, though torn apart,
In the stitching lies the art.
Every whispered word a seam,
Holding tight to every dream.

Loosely woven, yet we fight,
In the dark, we search for light.
Through the struggles, love will mend,
Frayed connections, souls transcend.

Though the fabric may grow thin,
In our hearts, we still begin.
With every tear, we learn to dance,
Threading love in every chance.

A Journey Through Echoing Hallways

In shadows cast by whispering walls,
Footsteps linger where silence calls.
Each corner hides a tale untold,
Memories dance in the faint and bold.

Windows frame a fleeting light,
Guiding souls through the quiet night.
Echoes bounce off aged stone,
In longing hearts, they find a home.

Time ventures forth, both swift and slow,
Each hallway leads where dreams may go.
Past the doors, a world ignites,
In the stillness, adventure invites.

With every turn, a breath we take,
Through forgotten paths, alive we wake.
Every echo beckons us near,
In the maze of our dreams, we steer.

So onward we tread in twilight's grace,
Through hallways where shadows embrace.
In this journey, let us roam,
For in the echoes, we find our home.

Puzzles of Unfinished Sentences

Words linger softly in the air,
Unfinished thoughts that lead to nowhere.
Fragments twist like autumn leaves,
In the silence, a heart believes.

Each pause a puzzle, deep and wide,
Stories wait, no place to hide.
Expressions tangled in the mind,
A search for meaning, hope defined.

With ink-stained hands and eyes that strain,
We chase the words through joy and pain.
Each sentence starts but fades away,
Leaving echoes of what we can't say.

In the gaps, our spirits clash,
Finding rhythm in the unspent cash.
These puzzles shape our very souls,
Embracing the chaos that makes us whole.

So let us dance in this brief light,
Solving riddles in the quiet night.
For every pause holds hidden grace,
In unfinished tales, we find our place.

The Veil of Nostalgia

A tender veil drapes over time,
Dancing lightly in rhythm and rhyme.
Faded pictures in memory's haze,
Whispering tales of golden days.

In quiet corners where shadows weep,
Old secrets stir from their slumbered sleep.
Each moment a fragrance, sweet and rare,
Wraps around us like a woven prayer.

Through windows misted with gentle tears,
We catch reflections of distant years.
A child's laughter, a lover's gaze,
All woven tightly in nostalgia's maze.

Time's river flows, yet stays the same,
Restoring warmth to every name.
In echoes soft, we find our way,
Where the heart remembers, love will stay.

So let us wander through this dream,
In the golden glow of memory's beam.
For in nostalgia, we find our truth,
A timeless bond to our lost youth.

The Language of Old Letters

In a drawer, they quietly lie,
Old letters penned with a sigh.
Each word a fragment of a soul,
In faded ink, they tell a whole.

Sealed in envelopes worn and frayed,
Love and loss, each carefully laid.
Promises whispered in quiet nights,
Captured moments, heart's delights.

Pages yellowed with the weight of time,
Echoes of laughter, stories in rhyme.
In every stroke, a heartbeat beats,
History lives in the things we repeat.

Unfolding secrets from years gone by,
As we read, emotions fly high.
Through the language of those written lines,
We uncover the pulse of sacred signs.

So cherish the words that softly flow,
In old letters, memories grow.
For every script holds a piece of art,
A timeless truth from the heart.

Fractals of Affection

In whispers soft, we intertwine,
Patterns swirl in love's design.
Each glance, a tale of something bright,
In colors bright, we paint the night.

Moments shared like fractals grow,
Infinite paths where feelings flow.
A touch, a laugh, a silent plea,
We dance together, wild and free.

Through storms we find our sacred ground,
In the chaos, love's pulse is found.
With open hearts, we face the day,
In every breath, we find our way.

Layers deep, our stories spin,
In this maze, we lose and win.
A mirror's edge reflecting truth,
In depths of youth, we find our roots.

Fractals weave our fate defined,
Complex patterns that bind, unwind.
In the tapestry, we leave our trace,
Forever etched in time and space.

The Echo Chamber of Memories

In shadows cast, our voices rise,
Echoing past beneath the skies.
Fragments linger, soft and clear,
In silent halls, I hold you near.

Each laughter shared, a cherished glow,
In corners where the soft winds blow.
Whispers dance, like leaves in flight,
In slumber's grasp, we find the light.

Faded photographs, stories told,
Reflections bright, our hearts unfold.
In lanterns flicker, time prevails,
Each memory etched in whispered tales.

The echo chamber, where we meet,
In rhythmic beats, our hearts repeat.
With every pulse, the past aligns,
In this space, your spirit shines.

As days draw close, the echoes swell,
In twilight's grace, our secrets tell.
A journey marked by laughter's song,
In the echo chamber, we belong.

The Scent of Worn Pages

In quiet nooks, the stories dwell,
With every turn, a magic spell.
The scent of words, both old and new,
Each page a world, a view askew.

Candlelight dances, shadows play,
As whispered tales drift far away.
In leather-bound dreams, we take flight,
With every line, the heart ignites.

Stories linger in every crease,
In the library's hush, we find peace.
The scent of ink, the touch of time,
In every verse, a gentle rhyme.

Faded edges, tales unfold,
In pages worn, our hearts consoled.
Each chapter waits, a new embrace,
In the scent of worn, familiar space.

With every book, a journey flows,
In curling pages, wisdom grows.
The stories woven, hearts entwined,
In the scent of words, our souls aligned.

Withering Daisies in Twilight

As daylight fades, the daisies sigh,
In twilight's grasp, they whisper why.
Petals droop in evening's glow,
A fleeting dance, a soft hello.

Time's gentle hand begins to weave,
In hues of gold, we learn to grieve.
Each flower's bend, a tale of grace,
In withering form, we find our place.

Their beauty lingers, though they fade,
In quiet moments, memories invade.
The twilight holds their fragile song,
A reminder that we all belong.

With every breath, a moment shared,
Amidst the dusk, we feel prepared.
To cherish life, both bright and dim,
In withering blooms, love's chances slim.

As night descends, the stars appear,
In darkness rich, we hold what's dear.
Withering daisies in the night,
In twilight's hug, we find the light.

Ribbons of Fleeting Happiness

In a garden where laughter blooms,
Ribbons dance in the gentle wind.
Moments wrapped in soft sunshine,
Fleeting, yet they leave a grin.

Through whispers of the morning light,
Joy flows like a babbling brook.
Each little smile, a spark ignites,
In pages of a storybook.

Colors blend in the twilight haze,
Every heart knows its hidden song.
Life paints joy in soft, warm rays,
Even when the day feels long.

Chasing shadows, we laugh in tune,
With every step, a memory grows.
Underneath the playful moon,
Time's gentle ebb, our spirit knows.

In ribbons worn by the gentle breeze,
Happiness lingers, sweet and brief.
We gather moments, wild like trees,
Embracing joy, letting grief leave.

Songs of the Unsaid

In silence lies a quiet strain,
Words unspoken guide our hearts.
A melody we can't explain,
Pulling threads as the night departs.

Hidden glances, subtle sighs,
Conversations beyond mere sound.
A world blooms beneath our eyes,
In the silence, love is found.

Songs of the unsaid, softly play,
Notes woven in the rafters high.
Each thought a line in our ballet,
Echoes linger, never die.

Across the chasm, souls connect,
Where silence speaks more than a word.
In that space, we both reflect,
Understanding waits, undeterred.

As dawn breaks, we hear them clear,
The sentiments that linger deep.
In the whispers, love draws near,
In the silence, secrets keep.

Beneath the Starlit Remnants

Underneath the vast expanse,
Starlight dances on the waves.
Lost in dreams, we take a chance,
Where the whispering night behaves.

Fragments of the past take flight,
Softly held in a midnight sigh.
Memories twinkle, oh so bright,
Glimmers of what once passed by.

Darkness drapes us like a cloak,
Embracing secrets we can keep.
In shadows shared, our hearts evoke,
Promises from the night's deep sweep.

With each flicker, stories breathe,
As constellations weave and spin.
Beneath the stars, we both believe,
In the tales where love begins.

As dawn approaches, starlights fade,
Yet the memory lingers on.
In the quiet, our hearts parade,
Holding tight to the starlit dawn.

The Diary of Hidden Affection

In a corner, dust gathers high,
A diary locked with careful care.
Pages filled with a soft sigh,
Secrets of love hidden there.

Ink flows like a gentle stream,
Wishes penned in a careful hand.
Each word a fleeting, wistful dream,
Charting feelings we can't understand.

Underneath the moon's pale gaze,
Desire hums upon the line.
In soft shadows, our stories blaze,
Love's quiet thrill, so divine.

Every chapter, a blush revealed,
Emotions caught in a fleeting glance.
Unfolding truths, our heart concealed,
In each phrase, a secret dance.

When the world fades to a hush,
Those pages whisper, soft and sweet.
In the stillness, feelings rush,
And the diary's heartbeat meets.

Withered Petals of Affection

In gardens where love once bloomed bright,
Now silence reigns, shadows in flight.
Petals fall, dreams begin to fade,
Memories linger in the glade.

Whispers of laughter, soft and sweet,
Echo through paths where we used to meet.
With each breath, the time slips away,
Holding tight to what was, come what may.

Love letters crumpled, tucked in drawers,
Time-worn pages with open doors.
Each tear a river, each smile a spark,
In the twilight glow, we leave our mark.

Once vibrant hues, now soft and grey,
In the quiet dusk of a fading day.
Promises linger in the secret air,
As I trace your name with trembling care.

Yet hope is a seed, in the heart's core,
Nurtured with dreams of forevermore.
Though withered petals may fall and part,
The scent of affection lives in the heart.

Silence Wrapped in Time

In the stillness, where shadows blend,
Time whispers softly, an unbroken friend.
Moments freeze, like fragile glass,
Holding echoes of the hours that pass.

A clock ticks gently in the night,
While memories dance in the pale moonlight.
Each second stretches, then swiftly flows,
Wrapped in silence, where no one knows.

Thoughts like clouds drift from my mind,
Floating softly, yet hard to find.
In the depths of quiet, the heart takes flight,
Seeking solace in the depths of night.

Seasons change, yet here I reside,
In the stillness, where secrets hide.
Each breath a chapter in a timeless tale,
Caught in the still, where words unveil.

The tapestry woven from silence and dreams,
Reveals the beauty in muted gleams.
Here in the echoes, we find our place,
Silence wrapped in time, a warm embrace.

The Canvas of Shared Glances

In crowded rooms, our eyes would meet,
In silent moments, where lives repeat.
Each glance a brushstroke, colors collide,
Painting stories where hearts confide.

Beneath the chatter, a world unseen,
In fleeting looks, what could have been.
Every twinkle, a spark in the air,
A canvas we crafted with exquisite care.

With shadows flickering, time stretches wide,
In the gallery of love, we take our stride.
A masterpiece etched in hearts and eyes,
Where dreams are held and never die.

Two souls entwined in a simple stare,
In moments of silence, we're laid bare.
Each heartbeat synchronized, a dance we find,
The canvas of life, vivid and kind.

Easel of thoughts and colors ablaze,
In the gallery of time, we wander and gaze.
With each shared glance, our journey unfolds,
A beautiful story that never grows old.

A Diary of Fading Sunsets

In the twilight whispers, pages turn,
Chasing shadows, as soft lights burn.
Each sunset captured in fragile lines,
A diary kept where the heart defines.

Colors bleed into the evening sky,
As moments linger and softly sigh.
Each chapter written in golden hues,
With words of wonder, love, and blues.

Fading echoes of laughter reside,
In the corners where memories abide.
We danced in the amber glow of dusk,
Chasing dreams wrapped in twilight's husk.

The ink of time flows on the page,
Every sunset, another stage.
In the twilight's embrace, we find release,
A diary filled with whispered peace.

So let the sun dip, let the stars ignite,
In the heart's diary, each fading light.
For even as day turns to night's embrace,
The sunset's beauty will never erase.

The Weight of Unspoken Promises

Silent whispers linger in the air,
Dreams unvoiced, heavy with despair.
Words unsaid, like shadows they creep,
Bound by the secrets we bury deep.

In the stillness, echoes of our fears,
Countless moments blurred by unshed tears.
Each promise hangs, an anchor in flight,
Yearning for truth, cloaked in the night.

The heart grows weary, burdened with fate,
Desires untouched, a haunting weight.
In the silence, we wrestle with blame,
Love unexpressed, forever the same.

Yet in the quiet, a flicker ignites,
Hope in the dark, a whisper of light.
With courage, we rise, ready to break,
The chains of the past, for love's sweet sake.

Together we stand, hearts open wide,
No longer lost, we turn the tide.
Unspoken no more, our voices combine,
The weight lifted, a new path to find.

A Dance in the Twilight

Beneath the dusk, where shadows play,
We twirl in silence, the end of the day.
Stars awaken, the sky painted gold,
A dance of dreams, in secrets untold.

Whispers soft as the night draws near,
Each step a promise, each glance sincere.
With every heartbeat, the world fades away,
In the twilight glow, together we sway.

The moonlight bathes us in silvery grace,
In this hushed moment, we find our place.
Lost in the rhythm of time standing still,
Every breath shared, a lingering thrill.

Around us, the gentle evening sighs,
As laughter fades into soft lullabies.
We waltz through the night, two souls intertwined,
In the dance of twilight, pure love defined.

When dawn breaks the spell, we'll see it through,
With memories tucked in the morning dew.
A dance everlasting, in hearts we'll keep,
In the twilight whispers, our love runs deep.

Hearts Woven in Time

In the fabric of life, our threads intertwine,
Stitched with the moments that sparkle and shine.
Every laugh shared, every tear that we weep,
A tapestry formed, our love we will keep.

Through seasons of change, we weather the storm,
In the warmth of embrace, we find our true form.
Memories crafted, a quilt soft and wide,
Together we journey, with love as our guide.

The years bend like branches, but roots hold us fast,
In the garden of time, our love will outlast.
Each heartbeat a stitch, each kiss a design,
In this life we've woven, your heart is in mine.

As the clock keeps its rhythm, we dance hand in hand,
With dreams like wildflowers, together we stand.
Though moments may fade, our love will endure,
In the fabric of time, forever secure.

Through laughter and sorrow, through thick and through thin,
The story of us, in the wind will begin.
For hearts woven in time are eternally wise,
In the tapestry of life, our love never dies.

The Ghosts of Warm Embrace

In the chill of the night, shadows take flight,
Ghosts of the past whisper soft in the light.
Once warm embraces now linger as sighs,
Memories haunt where true love never dies.

Familiar laughter dances on the breeze,
Echoes of moments that brought us to knees.
Each memory paints a smile and a tear,
The past holds its breath, and we still feel near.

Through the veil of the night, your presence I crave,
A warmth that remains from the heart that you gave.
In the silence that follows, your spirit still plays,
In dreams we are dancing, despite the delays.

Yet time is a thief, and seasons may change,
The warmth of your touch feels forever estranged.
Though life may divide, love's essence remains,
In the ghost of your arms, I still know no chains.

So here in the dusk, I embrace what was true,
With every soft whisper, I'm still close to you.
The ghosts of our warmth will forever entwine,
In the tapestry woven, our souls intertwine.

The Sweet Sorrow of Echoing Footsteps

In quiet halls where shadows tread,
Whispers linger, softly spread.
Footsteps fade on dusty floors,
Memories call from distant shores.

Each step a story, softly told,
Of laughter shared, of hands to hold.
Yet silence wraps like morning mist,
In every echo, a gentle twist.

Time weaves threads of joy, of pain,
In every hollow note, a gain.
The sweet sorrow, a dance of sighs,
As echoes whisper, love never dies.

In the twilight where shadows blend,
Footsteps linger, paths may wend.
Though they fade, their warmth remains,
In my heart, love's soft refrains.

So with each echo, I find grace,
A tender heart knows its place.
In sweet sorrow, I find my peace,
Footsteps echo, but never cease.

Flickering Flames of Past Encounters

Upon the hearth, the embers glow,
Flickering flames, the stories flow.
Each spark a moment, rich and bright,
A dance of shadows in the night.

Faces flash in the yellow light,
Laughter dies but spirits ignite.
In every flicker, warmth is found,
Connections lost, yet love surrounds.

The crackling wood sings of the past,
Moments cherished, forever cast.
Time may dim the brightest flame,
But memories burn, never the same.

Whispers linger in the air,
Echoes of joy, a sweet affair.
Flickering flames, a heart's embrace,
In the stillness, we find our place.

With every glow, our spirits rise,
In past encounters, love belies.
Fleeting moments, forever seam,
Flickering flames, our shared dream.

In the Garden of Lost Petals

In the garden where dreams once bloomed,
Petals fall, their colors consumed.
Whispers of beauty linger near,
Among lost petals, I find my fear.

Each flower tells a tale untold,
Of love's embrace, of days of gold.
Yet time, the thief, has claimed them all,
In the silence, I hear their call.

The fragrance fades, a bittersweet trail,
Each withered bloom, a winding tale.
In shadows cast by trees above,
The garden holds what once was love.

Yet in loss, there's a spark of light,
Memories dance in the velvet night.
Amidst lost petals, hope remains,
In the garden, love's sweet pains.

So I wander through this sacred space,
Embracing loss with gentle grace.
In every petal's soft decay,
A reminder that love finds its way.

An Echo of Heartbeats

Beneath the stars, two hearts align,
In whispered dreams, their fates entwine.
Echoes of pulses, soft and low,
A symphony of love's warm glow.

In quiet moments, silence speaks,
Each heartbeat mirrors what love seeks.
A gentle rhythm, strong and true,
An echo of what we both pursue.

Through trials faced and joy embraced,
In every touch, our souls are graced.
The echoes linger, rich and deep,
Awake in dreams, while others sleep.

Though distance tries to pull apart,
The echo finds its way to heart.
In every beat, we find our song,
Together, where we both belong.

So let the echoes guide our way,
Through night and dawn, through dusk and day.
An echo of heartbeats, ever near,
In love's embrace, we cast out fear.

Echoes of Heartstrings

In the silence, whispers roam,
Through the chambers of our hearts.
Every echo, a cherished tome,
Binding us, though life departs.

In laughter's glow, memories dance,
Fleeting shadows that remain.
An unwavering, sacred chance,
Love's imprint, a sweet refrain.

Time flows like a gentle stream,
Carving paths in distant sands.
Yet in dreams, we weave a dream,
Hand in heart, through distant lands.

Silent promises held tight,
Beneath a starry, velvet sky.
In the stillness of the night,
Love's soft echoes never die.

Forever bound, two hearts entwined,
In this dance of light and shade.
In every beat, the ties defined,
The echoes of love, unafraid.

Shadows of Affection

In twilight's soft and tender glow,
Two silhouettes begin to blend.
With whispered words, our secrets flow,
In shadows where our hearts ascend.

The quiet breeze knows how we feel,
As dreams take flight on gentle wings.
In every glance, a silent deal,
Where affection softly sings.

We walk where time has lost its name,
In the stillness, we reside.
With every heartbeat, love's acclaim,
As shadows dance, our worlds collide.

Through the veil of dusk, we find,
A solace in our tender gaze.
In every touch, the ties remind,
Of fleeting hours and endless days.

With hands entwined, we face the dawn,
In the warmth of light's embrace.
Though shadows fade when night is gone,
Affection leaves a lasting trace.

The Fragrance of Reminiscence

In a garden where memories bloom,
Petals whisper tales of old.
Each scent evokes a sweet perfume,
In the heart, love's stories told.

Time drifts like petals on a breeze,
Carrying hints of laughter shared.
In every corner, the heart sees,
Echoes of moments, unprepared.

The soft rustle of leaves above,
Sings songs of whispers softly spun.
In quietude, we feel the love,
As sunlight warms the day begun.

With every breath, nostalgia swells,
In colors bright, the past resounds.
In fragrant notes, our spirit dwells,
Binding our hearts in timeless rounds.

So let us linger, lost in grace,
In every scent that drifts our way.
For in this fragrant, sacred space,
We hold our yesterdays at bay.

Tattered Pages of Us

In a book where stories weave,
The chapters sing of love once bright.
Each tattered page, a tale we leave,
In the shadows of gentle night.

Ink stains tell of laughter spilled,
Moments etched in faded dreams.
With every word, a heart fulfilled,
In the silence where hope gleams.

Through tangled lines, our souls converse,
In whispers held by ink's embrace.
Each curve and twist, a universe,
Where time entwines with love's soft trace.

Though pages fray and times may change,
The essence of us lingers near.
In every chapter, love can range,
In every sigh, our truth sincere.

So let us write, though storms may gust,
In ink of gold, our hearts will trust.
For in this story, it's just us,
Tattered pages, love is a must.

A Tapestry of Once Upon a Time

In the quiet glow of evening light,
Stories whisper through the air,
Dreams of castles, dragons in flight,
Lives entwined in a vibrant fair.

Threads of laughter, joy, and pain,
Woven tightly, fragile yet strong,
Each memory a soft refrain,
Echoing in the hearts all along.

Chasing stars as dusk descends,
Children play in fields of gold,
Time and space forever bends,
As the tales of old are told.

In shadows dance those we cherish,
Embers flickering, fading slow,
Though seasons change and faces perish,
The essence lingers, love's warm glow.

A tapestry with colors bright,
Reminds us of the hands that weave,
In every strand a spark of light,
A treasure trove for hearts to cleave.

The Imprints We Leave Behind

Footsteps tracing patterns in the sand,
Moments fleeting, etched in time,
Every heartbeat, a gentle strand,
Weaving tales in life's soft rhyme.

With every laugh, with every tear,
Imprints mark our journey's way,
Like whispers carried through the years,
A legacy in bright array.

In the forest, the branches sway,
Echoes of voices lost in thought,
Every choice a game we play,
Lessons learned and battles fought.

The shadows dance in fading light,
Casting memories upon the ground,
In the silence of the night,
Our stories linger, ever found.

So as we walk this path anew,
Let kindness guide the steps we take,
For in the end, it's love that's true,
The imprints left will never break.

Memories Wrapped in Soft Silence

In the hush of dawn's embrace,
Time stands still, the world awakes,
Gentle whispers, a tender trace,
Of laughter shared and love we make.

Faded photographs, soft and worn,
Capture moments, capturing grace,
From childhood's laughter, hearts reborn,
To distant dreams time can't erase.

Wrapped in silence, feelings swell,
Each glance a story, each touch a song,
In quietude, we seem to dwell,
Where echoes of the past belong.

Through golden fields where shadows play,
I hear your voice in every breeze,
Memories guide me on my way,
With every heartbeat, every ease.

So let us sit, hand in hand,
In soft silence, find our peace,
Where love's sweet whispers softly stand,
And memories forever increase.

The Journey from Here to What Was

A road unravels, stretching wide,
With every step, we ponder deep,
The road behind, a faithful guide,
With echoes of the past we keep.

Mountains climbed and valleys crossed,
Each lesson learned, a treasure gained,
In every moment, nothing lost,
The journey's flow, forever stained.

The skies may weep, the sun may shine,
Yet through it all our spirits soar,
Mapped in stars, our paths entwined,
Filling pages, forevermore.

From here to what was, we will roam,
With dreams alight, heartbeats aglow,
In every ending, we find home,
For in our minds, memories grow.

So take my hand, let's forge a way,
Together weaving tales anew,
The journey beckons, day by day,
From here to what was, me and you.

Echoes of Yesterday's Embrace

In twilight's glow, memories linger,
Faded whispers that softly sing,
The warmth of your touch, forever held,
In shadows where time escapes its ring.

Beneath the stars, our laughter soared,
Each heartbeat a promise, blissfully sweet,
With every glance, the world aligned,
In that fleeting moment, we were complete.

The dance of days, a gentle breeze,
Echoes of love, entwined like vines,
In the silence, our souls embraced,
A timeless bond that still defines.

Yet in the dawn, we drifted apart,
With dreams cast wide, like ships at sea,
The embrace of yesterday fades away,
But in my heart, you still sail free.

Now reflections of a sweet refrain,
In corridors where silence resides,
Life moves on, yet love remains,
An echo of us, through all tides.

Whispers Beneath the Stars

On starlit nights, our secrets twirled,
In moonlit glances, fate would mark,
With every sigh, the cosmos sighed,
Whispers woven in the dark.

Your laughter danced on the silver air,
As constellations sparked in flight,
Two souls adrift in the vast unknown,
Finding solace in shared delight.

The universe listened, hearts drew near,
While shadows played on ancient trees,
Each moment we held was etched in light,
A tender hymn carried by the breeze.

In dreams we met, where wishes lie,
And stars conspired to make us whole,
Our voices shared a timeless tune,
A lullaby to soothe the soul.

Yet dawn approached, the spell would break,
The world awoke, the magic faded,
But in the quiet, I hear your voice,
In whispers, forever serenaded.

Moments Etched in Heartstrings

In fleeting glances, moments gained,
A tapestry we wove with care,
Each heartbeat stitched with silken thread,
A love story, tender and rare.

From sunrise dreams to twilight sighs,
We painted skies with colors bright,
In every laugh, in every tear,
Memories danced, a soft delight.

The warmth of your hand, a sacred place,
Guiding me through the stormy nights,
In the chaos of life, we found our calm,
Holding tight through the darkest fights.

As seasons change, our canvas grows,
Moments etching deeper still,
Through laughter loud and whispers sweet,
We craft our fate with iron will.

In the twilight's hush, we sit side by side,
Replaying the love that forever clings,
Each heartbeat a note in life's grand song,
Moments etched in heartstrings.

The Aftertaste of Affection

In the sweetness of dawn, we lingered close,
The warmth of your heart, a cherished treasure,
With every glance, a soft embrace,
The aftertaste of love, pure pleasure.

As sunlight spilled through the window pane,
We danced to rhythms only we could hear,
In each fleeting sigh, a promise made,
A song of affection drawing near.

Yet time is a thief in the quiet night,
As shadows pass on a fleeting chance,
The taste of your love remains a muse,
A bittersweet essence in life's dance.

In memories held, your laughter plays,
Like notes of a tune, forever echoing,
In the aftertaste of those warmest days,
A melody of love forever flowing.

Though paths may stray, and seasons change,
The heart knows well what it cannot sever,
In the aftertaste of affection's glow,
We are timeless, and always together.

A Flickering Flame of Togetherness

In the shadow's gentle sway,
We find solace, come what may.
Hand in hand, dreams ignite,
Two souls dancing in the light.

With whispers exchanged in the night,
Laughter echoes, hearts take flight.
Every moment, a treasure we hold,
A love that's timeless, yet bold.

Through storms and trials, we stand strong,
In our embrace, we belong.
The world outside may fade away,
In each other's arms, we'll stay.

As seasons change and rivers flow,
Our bond continues to grow.
Like a flickering flame, so bright,
Together, we conquer the night.

In each heartbeat, a silent vow,
A sacred promise, here and now.
For love is a flame that will never tire,
Together, we rise, forever inspire.

The Bridge of Moments Lost

On the river of time we drift,
Each current holds a precious gift.
Memories fading, like mist at dawn,
Across the bridge, our dreams are drawn.

In laughter's echo, shadows play,
The past returns, and slips away.
With every step, a chapter closed,
Yet in our hearts, the story flowed.

Moments cherished, yet so brief,
Threads unravel, leaving grief.
The bridge we walk, both weak and strong,
Binds the melodies of our song.

But in the silence, we find the way,
To treasure each moment, come what may.
Though time may steal what we hold dear,
Love lingers on, forever near.

As we traverse this bridge of fate,
Together we learn to appreciate.
Though moments lost may haunt our dreams,
In unity, we weave our seams.

The Sounds of Yesterday Whispered

In twilight's hush, the echoes call,
Whispers of love, of rise and fall.
Through rustling leaves, and murmurs low,
The sounds of yesterday softly flow.

Each note a memory, sweet and clear,
Filling the silence, drawing us near.
A symphony of voices lost,
In the winds of time, a gentle cost.

The laughter shared, the tears we've shed,
The paths we traveled, the words unsaid.
In shadows cast by the setting sun,
The sounds of yesterday linger on.

In every heart, a story resides,
A melody that forever guides.
With each refrain, we find our way,
Embracing echoes of yesterday.

So let us listen, let us remember,
Through every season, each passing ember.
In the whispering winds, our souls entwine,
The sounds of yesterday, forever shine.

Requiem for a Forgotten Heart

In the silence where shadows dwell,
A heart once vibrant cast its spell.
Echoes of laughter, dreams once bright,
Fade into whispers of the night.

In the corners of time, memories weep,
Promises broken, secrets we keep.
A requiem plays for joy once known,
For love that blossomed, then overthrown.

Each beat a story yet untold,
Of warmth and passion, love, and cold.
In the stillness, a haunting sigh,
A forgotten heart learns to cry.

Yet hope lingers in dimmest light,
In shadows, a flicker, soft and slight.
From ashes, a new flame may rise,
Transcending the sorrow, reaching the skies.

A requiem sung, yet not the end,
For even the heartbroken can mend.
In the journey of loss, we find our part,
A resurrection from a forgotten heart.

Fragments of a Heartbeat

In the silence, whispers call,
Lost echoes dance and fall.
Fleeting moments, time apart,
Captured pieces of a heart.

Shattered dreams in softest light,
Glinting shards that heal the night.
A pulse beneath the fractured skin,
Telling tales of where we've been.

Every heartbeat, a story spun,
Of battles fought and battles won.
In the remnants, life prevails,
As love will weave through all the trails.

Memory's touch is bittersweet,
Missing pieces, yet complete.
In fragments, we still find our way,
Towards the dawn of a new day.

Mosaic of Past Promises

Once we stood on dreams so grand,
A future bright, a steady hand.
Promises held like precious glass,
Each one fragile, yet they last.

In every color, stories blend,
Shattered hopes that softly mend.
Every tile, a glimpse of time,
Crafting life's intricate rhyme.

Echoes linger, soft and clear,
Whispers of what we hold dear.
In the mosaic, love is found,
In silent vows that still resound.

Beneath the surface, layers grow,
Each experience, a vibrant flow.
A tapestry of where we've been,
In shades of laughter, tears, and sin.

Yet through the cracks, light shines bright,
A radiant dance in darkest night.
In our hearts, the art remains,
A testament amidst the chains.

Threads of Enchantment

Woven tightly, tales arise,
In the fabric, magic lies.
Golden threads and silver seams,
Stitching softly woven dreams.

In the twilight, shadows play,
Whispered secrets float away.
Captured moments in each fold,
Stories waiting to be told.

Through the loom, the heart will guide,
Binding hopes we cannot hide.
Each stitch a path, a whispered chance,
Inviting us to join the dance.

From a shroud of night, we weave,
Threads of joy, and love believe.
In the tapestry, we roam free,
Threads of enchantment, you and me.

And in the dawn, our patterns glow,
A tapestry that ebbs and flows.
Together woven, hand in hand,
An endless journey, a promised land.

The Ember of What Once Was

In the hearth of memory's blaze,
Flickering warmth of bygone days.
Softly glowing, yet so dim,
The ember's light, a tender hymn.

Through the shadows, whispers sigh,
Echoes from the firefly.
Once bright flames, now cooling ash,
Cast reflections of a past flash.

In the ashes, stories lie,
Of laughter, love, and goodbye.
Each spark a moment, a soft kiss,
In the ember, glimpses of bliss.

We gather round and share the light,
Rekindling dreams in the night.
Though time may dim the brightest flame,
The ember glows, calling your name.

Hold it close, let warmth remain,
In the heart, the ember's gain.
For what once was shall never fade,
In the stories, warmth is laid.

The Weight of a Thousand Unsaid Goodbyes

In shadows deep, we linger still,
Words untold, a heavy chill.
Silent nights bear witness true,
To the weight of love anew.

Eyes that meet, but never say,
Promises fade, lost in gray.
Hearts entwined in whispered sighs,
Holding tight, yet saying goodbyes.

Moments passed like fleeting dreams,
Echoes haunt with silent screams.
Every glance a story spins,
In the end, where silence wins.

Each unsaid word a burden held,
In the quiet, emotions swelled.
A thousand goodbyes left behind,
In the closeness, we are blind.

Yet in the heart, a ember glows,
A fire that only true love knows.
Though words may drift like setting suns,
The weight of love remains as one.

Tides of Emotion in Still Waters

Beneath the calm, a storm does brew,
Emotions rise, both old and new.
Still waters hide the raging fight,
A dance of shadows in moonlight.

Whispers brush against the shore,
Silent cries, we long for more.
Waves crash softly, then retreat,
Leaving traces of hearts that beat.

Memories swirl in eddies deep,
Secrets kept, in silence weep.
Tides of change pull us apart,
Yet bind the threads of every heart.

In stillness lies the tempest's core,
Yearning for what was before.
Every ripple tells a tale,
Of love that soared, yet chose to sail.

But in the depths, resilience grows,
Underneath, the current flows.
With every tide, we find our way,
Through still waters, come what may.

The Canvas of Remembered Touch

In every brush, a memory glows,
A touch, a spark, where love still flows.
Colors vivid, emotions bold,
On this canvas, our story told.

Fingers trace the lines of fate,
In soft strokes, we resonate.
A dance of hues, both light and dark,
Each stroke a whisper, each shade a spark.

Moments frozen, yet alive,
In the art where we survive.
Past and present intertwine,
In every layer, your heart and mine.

The canvas breathes, each fold and crease,
Telling tales of love's release.
Footprints linger, in paint and soul,
In this creation, we are whole.

As time unfolds a new design,
The art remains, a love divine.
With every brush, we leave our mark,
In the canvas, we ignite the spark.

Ripples in a Silent Sea

In the stillness, ripples spread,
A silent sea, where dreams are wed.
Softly gliding, whispers sway,
In the quiet, hearts find their way.

Layers deep beneath the calm,
Gentle tides, a timeless balm.
Every ripple tells a story,
Of love entwined, in all its glory.

Moonlit nights on tranquil waves,
Secrets carried, the heart enslaves.
In each surge, a memory flows,
In the depths, true love bestows.

Still the sea, yet alive with grace,
Reflecting dreams, a tender space.
The calm disguises the truth we seek,
In silent depths, our souls speak.

So let the ripples break the night,
In quiet waters, we find light.
For in the silence, we can see,
The beauty of love's mystery.

Time Capsules of Heartfelt Memories

In boxes dusty, dreams reside,
Each trinket holds a story wide.
Whispers echo, laughter rings,
Moments cherished, time still clings.

Old photographs in sepia tones,
Capture smiles, love's gentle moans.
Faded letters, ink now blurred,
Tell of feelings, softly stirred.

Broken toys and childhood games,
Tokens of love, still the same.
Each memory a thread we weave,
Timeless tales we can retrieve.

Through the years, we gently tread,
In heart's chambers, all is fed.
Time capsules hold what we can't lose,
Treasured moments, love infused.

In quiet hours, we reminisce,
Recalling joys too sweet to miss.
In every heart, a capsule stays,
Guarding love in countless ways.

Starlit Paths of Unspoken Words

Beneath the sky, our silence grew,
In every glance, a magic hue.
Unspoken dreams drift soft and light,
Guided by stars in the night.

The moon reflects our hidden thoughts,
In whispered breaths, connection's sought.
Each heartbeat echoes, loud and clear,
In starlit paths, we draw near.

Mirrored in eyes, a universe,
Words untold, a silent verse.
Hands brushed gently, sparks ignite,
A language formed in purest light.

Every star a wish we make,
In twilight's calm, our hearts awake.
No need for words, the sky understands,
With starlit paths, we leave our brands.

In the quiet, truth unveiled,
Through uncharted skies, love hailed.
Unspoken words, forever heard,
Bloom in silence, soothing, stirred.

When Laughter Fades, Silence Speaks

In shadows cast by fading light,
Where laughter danced, now hush feels right.
A gentle hush envelops near,
In somber tones, we hold what's dear.

The echoes of our joy once rang,
In vibrant tones, our spirits sang.
But as the laughter dims away,
Silence whispers what hearts can't say.

Memories linger, bittersweet,
In quiet moments, we retreat.
Though laughter fades, love remains,
In silent bonds, the heart gains.

Through tears and smiles, a tale unfolds,
Of life's embrace, both soft and bold.
When laughter fades, the truth will seek,
In the solace found, silence speaks.

Within the stillness, strength is found,
In every heartbeat, love's profound.
When laughter fades, let silence be,
The voice of love, eternally.

The Color of Nostalgic Dreams

In shades of blue and golden hues,
Nostalgic dreams sprinkle like dew.
Whispers of youth, soft and true,
Paint the sky in colors new.

Wandering paths through fields of gold,
In each step, a story told.
Time's palette shows what we embrace,
The colors of a timeless place.

Green of laughter, red of tears,
Every hue reflects our fears.
Brushstrokes gentle, love's warm gleam,
Each memory a vibrant dream.

In twilight's glow, the colors blend,
Past and present, closely mend.
Reflections dance in fading light,
Nostalgic dreams take flight tonight.

The canvas broad, our hearts the frame,
In every color, we find our name.
Embrace the hues that life redeems,
For a life well-lived is painted in dreams.

A Tapestry of Shared Silence

In quiet moments, we reside,
A tapestry woven, side by side.
Threads of whispers softly blend,
A bond unbroken, time won't bend.

Shadows linger, soft and deep,
In this silence, secrets keep.
Each heartbeat echoes, night and day,
In the hush, we find our way.

Fingers touch in fleeting grace,
An unspoken, sacred space.
The world fades, just you and I,
Underneath the endless sky.

With gentle sighs, we drift awhile,
In shared silence, we can smile.
No need for words; we understand,
Together here, we make our stand.

As the stars begin to glow,
A tapestry of love we sew.
In every thread, a story dwells,
In shared silence, magic swells.

A Journey Through Velvet Shadows

In velvet shadows, dreams take flight,
Through whispered paths of soft twilight.
The moonlight dances, shadows sway,
In midnight hues, we drift away.

Each step leads us deeper still,
Through secret woods, a gentle thrill.
Veils of night embrace our fears,
In quiet strength, we shed our tears.

Beneath the stars, we find our truth,
In velvet cloaks, we reclaim youth.
Through every turn, the heartbeats race,
In shadows warmed, we find our place.

The world behind us fades from view,
A journey shared, just me and you.
We weave our dreams where shadows play,
In velvet nights, we'll find our way.

The dawn awaits, but here, we stay,
In velvet shadows, we'll find our way.
With every breath, a promise blooms,
In twilight's embrace, love resumes.

Secrets Beneath the Surface

Beneath the waves, the whispers hide,
Secrets murmur with the tide.
In silent depths, the truth runs deep,
What lies beneath, we dare to keep.

Moonlight glimmers on the sea,
Shimmering visions, wild and free.
With every ripple, stories rise,
Secrets hidden beneath the skies.

Diving deep, we seek to find,
The buried hopes within the mind.
A treasure trove of dreams in seed,
Where silence tends to every need.

The ocean's heart, a world untold,
In shadows deep, we are bold.
What lies beneath, we'll brave the storm,
In changing tides, our love will warm.

With each wave, the truth unfolds,
Secrets beneath in whispers told.
A dance of light, a flicker bright,
In the depths, we find our light.

The Horizon of What Was

On the horizon, memories glow,
Whispers of what we used to know.
Echoes linger in the air,
A bittersweet taste, everywhere.

Sunset paints the sky in dreams,
Softly fading, or so it seems.
The past a canvas, rich and wide,
With each stroke, a gentle tide.

We navigate through soft goodbyes,
In the twilight, love never dies.
Each moment captured, held so dear,
In the shadows, you still are near.

The horizon beckons, bright and true,
A beacon calling, me and you.
With every dawn, we start anew,
In the echoes of all we've been through.

What was, still shapes the path ahead,
In the memories, we gently tread.
The horizon glows with light amassed,
In our hearts, the echoes last.

The Dialogue of Unravelling Threads

In shadows we speak, softly untwist,
The fabric of time, a delicate tryst.
Fingers brush gently, though words may evade,
Each silence reveals what the heart has laid.

We weave through the loom of our tangled past,
Echoes of laughter, memories cast.
Threads intertwine, forming patterns they share,
Yet beneath the surface, there's more laid bare.

The tapestry shifts with the pull of the night,
Glimmers of truth in the fading light.
With every unspooled story we tell,
The dialogue deepens, casting its spell.

In whispers we gather, the pieces align,
Stitching our stories, through love they entwine.
Each tug reveals what we often ignore,
A tender reminder of what's at the core.

As the last thread breaks, freedom's a gift,
Unraveling paths that once seemed adrift.
We honor the journey, the tales that we wove,
In the dialogue's close, our spirits now rove.

When Stars Align and Fade

In twilight's embrace, we find a soft glow,
Stars in their dance, gently whisper and flow.
Moments collide, like the night's sweet refrain,
When dreams cascade softly, as hopes intertwine.

We linger in silence, where wishes are spun,
Countless constellations, our journeys begun.
With each pulse of time, fate's rhythm confined,
The night sky a mirror of hearts intertwined.

Yet as dawn approaches, our visions may blur,
The stars, they grow dim, the cosmos may stir.
In the fading light, we still hold onto dreams,
For even in shadows, hope quietly gleams.

So cherish the moments when fate draws us near,
Embrace every heartbeat, surrender the fear.
For stars that align, though they drift far away,
Leave traces of magic that forever will sway.

As the day breaks anew, in golden embrace,
We carry the echoes, the light, and the grace.
Though stars may have faded, their warmth will remain,
In the tapestry woven, through joy and through pain.

The Color of Unspoken Words

In whispered hues, the palette displays,
The tones of our hearts in delicate ways.
Each glance a brushstroke, emotions run deep,
Where silence prevails, and secrets we keep.

The canvas of friendship, with shadows and light,
Draws figures of moments we treasure each night.
In laughter, in sorrow, the colors combine,
Creating a masterpiece, uniquely divine.

Yet still there lie shades that are rarely revealed,\nFrom
hearts through the silence, a truth is concealed.
The gray of the doubts, the bold strokes of fear,
Paint landscapes of stories we yearn to make clear.

But within every silence, a rainbow takes flight,
A spectrum of feelings emerges from night.
And though words may falter, the heart finds its way,
Through the color of unspoken, come what may.

So embrace every shade that defines who we are,
For even in darkness, we shine like a star.
In the gallery of life, may we always find peace,
In the beauty of silence, may our hearts find release.

Tangled Roots of Familiarity

In the garden of life, where friendships take root,
We find tangled branches that serve as our suit.
Each story entwined, a testament shared,
In the soil of memory, love's gently bared.

Time weaves its magic through laughter and tears,
Binding our fates through the passage of years.
With every new season, our bonds shift and grow,
Yet deep in the earth, familiarity flows.

We cradle the moments both bitter and sweet,
Nurturing love where the past and present meet.
In the shadows of doubt, we seek out the light,
Finding strength in each other, our spirits ignite.

Though storms may arise, and the winds may betray,
Together we flourish, come what may.
In roots that are tangled, we discover the grace,
Of nurturing hearts in this sacred space.

So let us embrace the connections we weave,
In the tapestry of life, it's love we believe.
Through tangled roots, may we joyously tread,
In the garden of friendship, where souls are fed.

Petals in the Wind

Petals dance beneath the sky,
Carried softly, they drift and fly.
Whispers of spring in the gentle breeze,
Nature's art, a heart at ease.

Colors swirl and fade away,
A fleeting moment, come what may.
Each one tells a tale of grace,
A memory made, a cherished space.

The sunbeams kiss the blooming ground,
In this beauty, joy is found.
Every petal holds a dream,
In the flow, we flow like stream.

Beneath the trees, shadows play,
As day turns slowly into gray.
A quiet peace, we take a stand,
In the petals, life is planned.

When the wind calls, we shall roam,
In each drift, we find our home.
Together, free, in soft ascend,
With petals in the wind, we blend.

Stories Untold

In the corners of the mind,
Whispers of a past designed.
Unwritten pages wait for light,
Hidden tales in the heart's sight.

Faded maps that guide the way,
Memories lost in yesterday.
Each breath holds a secret dear,
A saga lost but always near.

Through the silence, voices call,
Their echoes rise, then gently fall.
In shadows, dreams take flight,
Beneath the stars, they reunite.

With every glance, we find the thread,
Of lives we lived, of words unsaid.
A tapestry of hopes and fears,
We weave the past through laughter, tears.

So listen close, the tales implore,
Unlock the heart, let spirits soar.
In stories untold, we find our place,
A journey shared, a boundless space.

Serendipity in the Rearview Mirror

In the twilight of a fading day,
Memories flicker, then drift away.
In the rearview, fate unfolds,
Serendipity's warmth, a story told.

Each mile traveled, a twist of fate,
Paths crossed by love without debate.
Moments fleeting, yet so profound,
In the journey, joy is found.

Time moves on, but echoes stay,
Sparks of laughter along the way.
The smiles shared, the hugs we gave,
Reflecting in the heart, they wave.

Chasing sunsets, we find the light,
Guided by dreams that shine so bright.
In the mirror, the past is clear,
Serendipity, a treasure dear.

As the road bends, we carry on,
With every moment, a new dawn.
Looking back at the trails we roam,
In the rearview mirror, we find home.

Threads of Time Touched by Heart

Threads of time, woven tight,
Stitching stories in the night.
With every heartbeat, a design,
Crafted softly, so divine.

Hand in hand, we share the path,
Building memories in love's warm bath.
Moments tangled, entwined with care,
In the fabric, dreams we share.

The loom of life, it spins and sways,
In the light of longest days.
Fleeting moments, echoes ring,
In the heart, the memories cling.

Through the ages, colors blend,
Every stitch, a story penned.
These threads of time, forever bold,
Touched by hearts, a tale unfolds.

As seasons change, the weft remains,
Woven love in joy and pains.
In the tapestry, we play our part,
Threads of time, touched by heart.

Footprints in the Sand of Yesterday

Footprints linger on the shore,
Memories washed, but not no more.
Each step taken, a moment lived,
In the sands, the heart's archives.

Waves roll in, erase the trail,
Yet in our minds, they tell a tale.
Whispers of joy, laughter bright,
In the sands, we found our light.

Sunset hues paint the sky,
While together, we dream and sigh.
Those footprints hold our sweetest days,
In every grain, our spirit stays.

As the tide pulls, we do not fade,
For in our souls, the journeys made.
With every breeze, we drift and sway,
Footprints in the sand, here to stay.

When morning breaks, we rise anew,
While past and present weave our view.
In every wave, a love confessed,
Footprints echo, forever blessed.

Unfolding Pages of a Silent Novel

In the quiet of the night, pages turn,
Whispers of stories waiting to be learned.
Faded ink, a tale of dreams and fears,
Memories etched, through laughter and tears.

Corners dog-eared, secrets laid bare,
Each line a heartbeat, a lingering stare.
Time pauses gently, a breath, a sigh,
Beneath the stillness, the echoes lie.

Chapters forgotten, yet still feel alive,
In shadows of silence, old worlds thrive.
A protagonist wanders, lost in thought,
With every epiphany, wisdom is sought.

Ink runs like rivers, thoughts intertwined,
In the story unfolding, what will we find?
Journey through pages, a map of the heart,
In the silence, the novel plays its part.

As dawn breaks softly, new light on the tale,
The end of this chapter won't let us fail.
For in every ending, a beginning waits,
Shaping the legacy that love creates.

Melodies of What We Used to Be

In a room full of echoes, notes drift on air,
Familiar refrains sing of moments we share.
Whispers of laughter, soft shadows of light,
Melodies linger, in the heart they ignite.

Time weaves a tapestry, melodies sweet,
Footsteps in rhythm, two souls in retreat.
Strands of the past, woven with care,
Each note a memory, a love laid bare.

Underneath stars, our voices will rise,
Caught in the magic, beneath midnight skies.
Songs of our youth, so carefree and bright,
Dance with the shadows, enveloped in night.

Yet time is a thief, as seasons unfold,
Leaving behind the stories untold.
Harmonies fade, but our hearts still sing,
In the silence of distance, hope is the spring.

As the sun sets gently, and dreams are set free,
Let's cherish the echoes of what used to be.
Within every heartbeat, a song will persist,
In melodies woven, love's never missed.

Fragments of an Unfinished Symphony

In the silence, a tune lies waiting to play,
Notes scattered like stars in the vastness of gray.
Each pause a heartbeat, a longing within,
A canvas of sound where the dreams begin.

Orchestras whisper tales of what could be,
Melodies haunting, like shadows at sea.
With every crescendo, emotions will swell,
A story unfolding, a heart's silent yell.

Strings hum softly, while the winds softly sigh,
Fragments of longing, like clouds drifting by.
In the silence, a promise still yearns,
For in every silence, the music returns.

Yet the symphony halts, caught in the breeze,
Moments suspended, like leaves on the trees.
Half-finished anthems cry out from the soul,
Incomplete, yet perfect, as it takes its toll.

The beauty of chaos, the grace in the flaws,
A dance of the notes, without any cause.
In the heart of the unfinished, hope's light will beam,
For here in the fragments, we dare to dream.

Vows Left Unsaid

In the quietest moments, words linger near,
Promises unspoken, hearts steeped in fear.
Soft glances exchanged, a language unique,
Vows left unsaid, but we both understand.

Between the pauses, love's rhythm beats strong,
A melody woven, where both souls belong.
In the hush of the night, intentions are clear,
Words may be absent, but the meaning is dear.

Yet life takes its course, on uncertain ground,
The longer we wait, the less we are found.
In the depths of longing, we search for the way,
Vows left unspoken, yet longing to stay.

With each fleeting moment, the chance drifts away,
What could have been often leads us astray.
Yet hope like a beacon, flickers in light,
In vows left unsaid, love ignites the night.

So here in the silence, a promise remains,
In the shadows of love, where no one complains.
For even unspoken, our truths will abide,
In the depths of the heart, where the vows still reside.

The Hearth of Passing Moments

In the glow of dusk's soft light,
Memories dance, taking flight.
Each flicker sways with grace,
Time's embrace leaves a trace.

Beneath the warmth of gentle flames,
Life's fleeting joy, it claims.
Stories whispered, tales unsaid,
In every heart, they thread.

Though shadows stretch, they do not bind,
For love's the flame we seek to find.
Moments melt like candle's wax,
In their glow, time never lacks.

Each heartbeat marks a vibrant song,
In the hearth where we belong.
Within the circle, laughter spills,
Sharing dreams and heartfelt thrills.

As embers fade in the night air,
We hold each memory with care.
These moments, although they flee,
Forever dwell in you and me.

When Echoes Form a Chorus

Whispers linger in the air,
Soft melodies, pure and rare.
Voices rise like morning mist,
In the silence, dreams persist.

A heartbeat sounds, then fades away,
Reverberates through night and day.
Together they weave a soft refrain,
In harmony, joy and pain.

Footsteps echo down the hall,
Carried by the night's soft call.
Each note a memory steeped in time,
A symphony in whispered rhyme.

In the corridors of our minds,
Where laughter, love, and sorrow binds.
The past unfolds in every sound,
Where echoes form, we're always found.

So listen close to the echoes' tale,
In the quiet where dreams sail.
For in each note, life's sweetness flows,
When echoes sing, the heart knows.

The Palette of Yesterday's Sunsets

Across the sky, the colors blend,
Crimson hues that twist and bend.
Each stroke, a story from the past,
In fading light, memories cast.

Golden rays touch the earth below,
Where whispered secrets softly flow.
Brushstrokes of lavender and gold,
Paint the tales that time has told.

As twilight gathers in the sky,
Shadows stretch, and day says goodbye.
A canvas holding joy and strife,
Each sunset sings of a shared life.

The palette shifts from dusk to night,
Reflecting dreams that took their flight.
In twilight's embrace, we find our way,
With colors bright to guide our stay.

So let us cherish each sunset's glow,
The rich hues of life we come to know.
For in each fading light's caress,
We find our peace, our happiness.

Whispers of Yesterday

In the silence, soft words weave,
Tales of hope, a gentle reprieve.
The echoes of laughter float,
With dreams and wishes, they emote.

Through the pages of time, they sway,
In glimpses of moments gone astray.
Each whisper holds a secret dear,
Of love and loss, of joy and fear.

In the rustle of leaves, they call,
A chorus shared by one and all.
From faded letters, stories rise,
Lighting the dark with their skies.

With every breath, they intertwine,
Whispers of grief and love align.
In the heart's chamber, soft they play,
Echoes of yesterday's ballet.

So let us listen to what they're saying,
In the whispers, life's ballet is swaying.
For in the past's gentle embrace,
We find our roots, our sacred space.

A Map of Past Encounters

In the shadows of memory, we stroll,
Tracing footsteps, stories untold.
Each face a chapter, each laugh a rhyme,
A tapestry woven, in the threads of time.

Places we lingered, soft whispers shared,
The warmth of connection, how deeply we cared.
Maps drawn in laughter, inked by the heart,
In moments unguarded, we each played our part.

Beneath the old oak, where secrets lay bare,
In gentle embrace, we breathed in the air.
With every encounter, a lesson we glean,
An ever-expanding, shimmering scene.

Yet time is a thief, it steals and it binds,
Fading those colors, blurring our minds.
But still, in our hearts, those moments remain,
Like stars in the night, eternal, unchain.

So here's to the faces that shaped who we are,
The map of our lives, each one a bright star.
Though paths diverge, and compass points stray,
The echoes of smiles forever will stay.

The Toll of Forgotten Lullabies

Hushed tones of slumber drift into air,
Whispers of dreams, woven with care.
The softest of melodies cradled our nights,
Now echoes of silence steal gentle delights.

Time calls the children, grown weary and wise,
Yet still we long for those tender goodbyes.
Lullabies linger, though voices grow faint,
Reminders of moments where love was the paint.

Forgotten, discarded, where once they would soar,
In the heart of the haunting, we long for them more.
A lull of the past, a bittersweet song,
In the threads of our being, they always belong.

Each note a reminder, each pause a regret,
The price of forgetting, a timeless debt.
Yet in quiet reflection, we hear them last,
Those lullabies ringing, resounding and vast.

So hold these lost whispers, so soft and so dear,
Remind us of childhood, of joy, and of fear.
For in every lullaby that rustles our dreams,
A piece of our hearts forever redeems.

Fleeting Glances, Lasting Imprints

A fleeting glance across the crowded room,
A spark ignites, dispelling the gloom.
An instant connection, a dance so divine,
In the depths of those eyes, a universe shines.

Moments like fireflies, bright in the night,
Breathless encounters, hearts racing in flight.
In silence we speak, emotions unfold,
The warmth of that look, far more than gold.

Yet time rushes onward, as shadows will chase,
The memories linger, in an ethereal space.
Each heartbeat a story, each look a new song,
In fleeting impressions, where we both belong.

Imprints of glances that linger and stay,
Marking our souls in a beautiful way.
Though moments may vanish, like dew in the dawn,
The essence remains, long after they're gone.

So cherish the fleeting, the brief and the rare,
For life is a canvas, painted with care.
With glances that shimmer, and love that won't fade,
In the heart of the moment, true magic is made.

Sunsets and Afterthoughts

The sky blazes orange, a fleeting display,
As daylight surrenders, giving night sway.
Each hue a reminder of moments we've lived,
In the canvas of twilight, our spirits are sieved.

We stand on the brink of the day's sweet goodbye,
Beneath the vast heavens that stretch and sigh.
Reflections arise in the calm of the dim,
As thoughts spill like colors, vibrant and grim.

The sun dips below, yet memories cling tight,
In shadows that dance, in the softening light.
Every sunset a promise, each dusk a new chance,
A time for reflection, a heartfelt romance.

We ponder the paths that our choices have made,
The dreams we have chased, and the plans that have frayed.
Yet in the afterthoughts, we find hidden grace,
In the colors of dusk, we each find our place.

So here's to the sunset, to endings and starts,
To the whispers of wisdom that echo in hearts.
In the beauty of twilight, embrace what you sought,
For life is a journey, adorned by our thoughts.

The Pulse of Old Melodies

In twilight's glow, the echoes rise,
Soft whispers dance beneath the skies.
Each note a tale, each chord a dream,
Old melodies flow like a gentle stream.

Faded voices, yet still they hum,
Beating hearts to a timeless drum.
Memories linger, wrapped in sound,
Where lost moments can still be found.

Through woven threads of harmony,
We find a glimpse of what used to be.
In every strum, a story told,
The pulse of music, timeless and bold.

Sifting Through the Ashes of Us

With every ember, a whisper glows,
A flicker of love that once arose.
We sift through the ashes, the remnants bare,
Finding pieces of moments we used to share.

The warmth of flames now turned to dust,
Yet in this heart, there's lingering trust.
Like shadows cast by a fading light,
We search for meaning in endless night.

Each spark a memory, fleeting and bright,
Against the backdrop of a starless night.
Our love once a fire, now a distant hue,
We sift through the ashes, seeking what's true.

The Unfinished Symphony of Hearts

In a quiet room, the silence swells,
An unfinished tune, where longing dwells.
Notes left hanging in the air,
A melody borne of love and despair.

Two hearts beat, a rhythmic chase,
Each pause a longing, each glance a grace.
In every silence, a story waits,
An unfinished symphony that captivates.

With every note, potential blooms,
In the shadows, love's contrast looms.
Though not complete, it sings so sweet,
The unfinished harmony of souls that meet.

Memories Etched in Moonlight

Beneath the moon, our secrets lay,
In whispers soft, they drift away.
Each silver beam a spark of grace,
Memories etched in time and space.

The night holds stories, rich and deep,
In every shadow, in dreams we keep.
Reflections dance on a still, dark lake,
Where whispered wishes softly wake.

In the cool embrace of evening's sigh,
We trace our footprints as time slips by.
With every breath, the past ignites,
Memories linger, carved in moonlight.

Remnants of Tender Touches

Fingers brush on soft skin,
A whisper lingers in the air.
Memories stitched with threadbare love,
Echoes of laughter without a care.

Glimmers of light through faded eyes,
Moments captured in a stolen glance.
The warmth of hearts, both intertwined,
Dancing softly in the quiet trance.

Every sigh a whispered confession,
Each heartbeat carries a silent song.
In the space where silence gathers,
The remnants of us still linger long.

Yet time erodes the finest silk,
Leaving shadows where we once stood.
But in dreams, tender touches remain,
Wrapped in stories we understood.

In the corners of our gentle past,
Memories like dust, refuse to fade.
Though the touch may not be present,
Its essence in our hearts is laid.

Shadows of Forgotten Romances

In twilight's embrace, love once bloomed,
Soft glances, now buried in mist.
Fleeting whispers, a tender sigh,
Leaving echoes we dare not resist.

Lovers' games played in secret nooks,
Hearts entwined by the moon's soft light.
Promises carved in the velvet dusk,
Fading softly, lost to the night.

Forgotten dances on weathered floors,
The touch of warmth lost in the breeze.
Every heart that loved and broke,
Now just shadows that float with ease.

Yet in the corners of worn-out dreams,
The flames of passion still faintly glow.
For every love that has slipped away,
The heart remembers, though it may not show.

Among the dust, there lies a glow,
Of tales untold, still yet to flow.
In the silence, the past remains,
Whispers of lovers, bound by chains.

Unwritten Letters in the Attic

In the attic's shadows, papers lie,
Untold words in a dusty nook.
Inkless pages of longing thoughts,
Silent secrets waiting to be took.

Each letter huddled, a story untold,
Dreams and wishes that never flew.
In the creases, time has folded hope,
The ink of fate choosing to eschew.

Ghostly musings hover in air,
A love that danced but never spoke.
In every tear, joy and despair,
Life's precious moments wrapped in cloak.

Voices whisper from forgotten dreams,
Carried on whispers of a breeze.
What could have been, one may ponder,
In the attic, wrapped in memories.

Yet in silence, a heart still beats,
For words unsaid are not erased.
Each unwritten letter waits for dawn,
To find the voice of love misplaced.

The Currency of Shared Secrets

In hushed tones shared beneath the stars,
Promises exchanged like fragile gold.
Every secret held like a treasure,
Bonding souls, brave and bold.

Whispers wrapped in the cloak of night,
Stolen moments where shadows meet.
The weight of trust, a delicate thread,
Binding hearts in silence sweet.

In the sanctuary of knowing smiles,
Laughter dances upon the breeze.
For every truth that lights the dark,
A secret shared brings hearts at ease.

Like currency forged in the fires of joy,
Every tale a gift that we keep.
In the tapestry of life we weave,
The threads of secrets run deep.

And as the dawn breaks over dreams,
The currency remains entwined.
For every secret between two souls,
Is a bond written in love's own kind.

The Architecture of Unbelief

In shadows deep where doubts reside,
A fortress built of whispers low,
Each brick a fear, each crack a sigh,
The heart debates, the mind says no.

Windows barred to light's embrace,
An echo chamber of the bold,
Where faith once danced, now silence lingers,
And dreams of truth turn cold.

The walls, they close, yet yearn to break,
For what if hope could carve a door?
Each glance outside, a silent ache,
What once was lost, could be restored.

Yet from the hearth, a spark can flare,
A whisper grows in shadows deep,
Could it ignite the embers there,
To lift the soul, from slumber steep?

In the architecture of the mind,
Where edifices of doubt stand tall,
A hidden path, a thread defined,
Could lead the heart beyond the wall.

A Garden of Withered Roses

In corners dark, the roses fade,
Their colors drained by endless nights,
Petals fall like memories made,
In silence lost, beneath the lights.

Once vibrant blooms, with scent divine,
Now crumbled dreams on midnight's floor,
A garden where the shadows pine,
And laughter echoes nevermore.

Yet nature whispers, life will find,
A crack to slip through, soft and slight,
In withered stems, new growth aligned,
Awaiting dawn's forgiving light.

Through tears of time, the soil heals,
As sun breaks forth, a gentle tune,
In every heart, a truth reveals,
That from decay, we'll rise, and bloom.

In this bleak earth, the hope resides,
For roses may wither, but hearts retain,
In tangled roots, the love abides,
Tomorrow's sun will break this chain.

Portraits of Heartfelt Solitude

In a quiet room, shadows play,
Portraits hung with tender care,
Each face a story, still as clay,
Whispers echo in the air.

An empty chair, a vacant seat,
Where laughter once filled up the space,
Now silence lingers, bittersweet,
Each glance a sigh, in time's embrace.

With every stroke, the colors blend,
A canvas rich with love and pain,
In solitude, the heart can mend,
Yet longs for touch, to break the chain.

In portraits framed, the memories stay,
A testament to moments shared,
Though time may steal, and dreams decay,
The heart remembers, unprepared.

So let each shadow tell its tale,
Of heartfelt bonds that never sever,
In solitude, we still prevail,
For love survives, now and forever.

The Weight of Yesterday's Tears

In silent nights, the tears cascade,
Each droplet holds a moment lost,
A weight that's born, a heart dismayed,
The price of love, a heavy cost.

Reflections dance on broken glass,
As echoes linger in the gloom,
What once was joy, now shadows pass,
And memories weave their own tomb.

Yet in the dark, a flicker glows,
A whisper of new dawn's embrace,
The weight of sorrow starts to pose,
A chance to rise, to find our grace.

For tears may fall, yet strengthen roots,
In fertile ground, the spirit grows,
With every drop, the soul computes,
Through all the hurt, new life bestows.

So hold the tears, don't turn away,
For yesterday's weight can set us free,
In the dawn's light, let shadows sway,
And find the strength in what will be.

Milton Keynes UK
Ingram Content Group UK Ltd.
UKHW022004131124
451149UK00013B/1005